A Sissy is Not the Man of the House

By Mistress Jessica

"So let me get this straight, you like putting on female undergarments, this evidently excites you and makes you feel naughty and erotic, and you want me to be part of this lifestyle that you so obviously enjoy"

"Does that about sum it all up sweetheart?"

I nodded my head, and lowered my eyes in a submissive way, I wasn't really sure how she was going to react to this whole thing but I knew it was now or never, which is why I had to tell her about my secret.

"Does this mean you are gay?" she asked

I looked up at her and into her eyes so that she knew I was telling her the truth.

"No I am not gay, I am not attracted to men, I am solely attracted to women." I explained to her.

She looked at me with that quizzical look on her face not sure to believe me or not.

I continued.

"It is the eroticism of being and doing something naughty that is my fetish, the fact that in our society it is looked down upon for men to wear stockings and panties makes it very erotic for me."

Again came the look but this time it also came with a bit of understanding, she herself had often enjoyed masturbating in the car while we were driving giving the truckers a look at her breasts, she told me it was exciting.

I brought that up as a final explanation of why I enjoyed doing what I was doing.

"Well then why do you want to bring me into it, you seem to be doing fine by yourself so far?" she followed with.

I didn't think it was fair of me to be keeping this secret from you and I certainly didn't want to have to explain myself to you if you were to catch me wearing something or came upon my stash of clothes one day.

She nodded her head at that as if to say damn straight I would have been pissed if I found some unknown panties lying around that were not mine.

"Well I don't have a problem with what you are doing if it makes you happy than knock yourself out I am not sure how I feel about being involved in your little games but I certainly won't stand in the way of it.

And with that it was said and it was done.

I would still keep my activities private and I was ok with that I just didn't want to face down a crazy woman if she came in to the bedroom while I was playing with myself and was wearing stockings and panties.

We were your average middle class couple we both worked nothing fancy but standard office jobs in the city, and had been married for about five years now and lived in a small apartment in the south part of the city, not the best part of town but certainly not the worst either.

Things continued as they had before, the cat was out of the bag but in reality it may have been before our conversation I am not really sure, but either way it was in the open between us about my panty wearing.

With that fact firmly rooted in my conscious I began to wear my panties more regularly. I didn't have that many since I only had worn them for masturbation sessions and then off they would come and cleaned and put away for the next time. I had always thought about expanding my set of panties to include many others in different collars and materials, but I had never had the opportunity to need more than the few pairs I had already and left it like that.

I had taken to wearing my panties as my normal underwear and quickly realized I needed to stop by the store on the way home from work. In a bold move to the furthering of my femininity I had decided that if I bought something feminine I would have to throw some masculine clothing item away in my sly attempt of feminizing myself.

That had always been the problem from the beginning I was trying to feminize myself for myself, it was like trying to be two different people at the same time, it was a very difficult task and at times often left me feeling like I was crazy or something. Of course I would concoct these elaborate mind bending twists and turns in an attempt to randomize the decision making process like if I lost at some game on the computer then I would have to wear my panties full time on the following day. This worked for the most part but in reality I knew I would have come up with some excuse to wear the panties anyway, I mean who was trying to fool here.

That night after work I stopped by the local department store and always felt so conspicuous as like the only man walking through the women's underwear department, sometimes I felt kind of creepy but other times I held my head proud, I got some looks but I stepped up to the cashier and felt the eyes of the customers behind me looking at me as the girl rang up the five pairs of very lacey and colorful panties up. I was pretty sure the girl behind the register knew they were for me, she had seen me buy other panties and stockings in the past. As I stepped away from the register with a bag of panties in hand I heard the cashier say something like. "I hope you enjoy your purchase"

Technically I guess she was the second person in the world to know I enjoyed a little cross dressing in my spare time.

It was after the first week of being a little panty slut that the second incident happened, I was on the computer on some social media site when my wife came in and dumped a pile of dirty panties in my lap.

"I don't think that it is fair for me to have to wash your dirty panties, you want a little more femininity in your life well let's give you a dose of the stereo typical view of a wife, from now on you can do your own laundry."

She didn't stick around for a response it was clear this had been decided well before she entered the room, and it was something I was expected to accept.

I picked up my panties and left the social media world for a bit and went about taking care of my knew responsibilities as a panty boy. I had helped with the laundry quite often so it wasn't such a large change of responsibility as things go, but now my panties were just out there in the open for all to see. The first time my wife came in the laundry room when I was folding my panties she just leaned against the doorframe and watched me, smiling she moved closer and soon was standing behind.

"Look at you folding your panties; it is so nice to see you taking care of your womanly things like that. I never saw you taking care of your male under garments in this fashion before. Her hand moved until it cupped my genitals and my rapidly hardening cock. Her hand sliding up and down beneath my balls, the silk of the panties that I had on against the skin of my cock was so amazing. She could see the difference in my reaction and it didn't take her long until her hand was inside of my pants and her own hand was now touching the front of my panties and she liked the silky feeling as her movements became even more vigorous. With her body pressed up against my own in a dominant position with her hand reached around my body putting me under her control.

"You have on a silky pair today don't you my little panty boy" she whispered in my ear.

"I am thinking I like you in panties, they make you so vulnerable, I like this feeling, I like the feeling of power this gives me over you."

I heard the words they were like a fire in my soul, they held me, and they made me feel different.

"Come on now panty boy, come on don't you want to cum in your panties for me?"

It didn't take much more convincing than that, I felt it well up inside of me as I pumped my load into the fabric of those panties.

"Well done panty boy."

She withdrew her hand from my pants.

"Oh look you shot your load through your panties and on my hand."

She raised it quickly and I soon found her hand pressed against my open mouth.

"Lick it off panty boy. Lick it off NOW."

Her words came out with a power in them that they did not have before and I felt a strong compulsion to obey them. Without thinking twice I had licked my cum from her hand it was just a small amount but it was like I was looking for her approval like it was necessary for my existence.

"Well done my little panty boy"

And just like that she just walked out of the laundry room. I finished up folding my clothes and went to put them away, and of course change out of the cum filled ones I had on.

The next day when I got home from work there was a very pretty paper bag like from one of those expensive stores, you know the ones that don't have price tags on the merchandise. Inside, wrapped in tissue paper was the most beautiful pair of panties I had ever seen. They were an off white silk I had never felt material such as this before, these were like the panties a new bride would wear on her wedding day.

I put them back daintily in the bag and put them away for a very special occasion.

*****

One Saturday found us in the shopping center in downtown; we had stopped for lunch and ended up in the department store. We always like to window shop you know seeing those things that were out for sale to make our lives more convenient. Of course convenience always came at a price, and those mechanical electronic devices were never a priority. We wondered through the clothing section and soon found ourselves in the women's department and then she dragged me into the underwear section. For some reason it felt much easier to be comfortable shopping for underwear with her there with me, and I never once felt like people were looking at me as touched and felt the fabric. I told her this and she thought it was quite amusing.

"Do you really think people look at you?"

"Well you know the mind can play tricks on you when you are excited." I told her.

She giggled at that again and began speaking with the sales girl. I wasn't paying attention to what they were saying as I continued to look at the under garments. I turned around and just caught the last part of the conversation.

"So you want me to measure your husband for a bra?" said the salesgirl

"Exactly" She smiled.

"Excuse me what was that." I responded.

"Oh stop it you know the natural next step for you is to have a proper bra to go with your panties." Said my wife out loud I might add for you to better understand the embarrassment.

As I began to voice my opinion she simply put her hand up and silenced me.

"Oh you have him well trained don't you" said the sales girl

I was about to say something about that but the hand was still in my face.

Next the sales girl was behind me forcing my hands up so she could slide the measuring tape around my chest.

"Oh look he is blushing" my wife said to the sales girl.

My senses were immediately heightened like when I am shopping alone in the woman's lingerie section, eyes seeking and searching to see if anyone was taking notice of me. Sure enough there were two young women and one was pointing in my direction, I was still trying to see if they were looking at me when my wife held up a very lacey bra to my chest. The second woman saw the whole thing and they both started to laugh as they continued to point in my direction.

It was my wife's hand upon my hard cock in my pants that brought me back to my own personal space.

"Well look at that a little embarrassment and your cock gets rock hard, that is an interesting little bit of information to know. " She smiled with an evil grin at this.

With the help of the sales girl they picked out a few different types and the sales girl went that extra mile and showed my wife what they had to make it look more realistic with regard to filling out the bra.

With five bra's in hand along with pads for that extra enhanced look I found myself in line at the cashier and who do you think would be in line in front of me but the two women that had seen me getting measured for the bras. I was going to move to another line but then I would have to explain to my wife why I wanted to do that.

"I will be right back; in fact I will meet you back at the car honey." She told me as she walked away.

It only took a moment before the women in front of me started up a conversation.

"I bet he is a gay, they must have one of those relationships I bet she is a lesbian as well."

"Are you gay or are you one of those secret cross dresser husbands" the woman asked.

I didn't even acknowledge they were speaking to me, just kept my eyes forward holding my soon to be new bras.

"Oh come on I read about men like you." She turned to her friend.

"You see they seem all normal on the outside but when they get home they change into women's clothes and enjoy doing the house work and other womanly chores all dressed up in dresses and stockings and high heel shoes, even makeup. Some of them like to wear women's undies under their man clothes during the day as well." She told her.

"Do you have panties on right now?" she turned and asked me.

I continued to look ahead even glanced at the all too familiar cashier who has seen me purchase panties on numerous occasions. I thought she would be the one to put these ladies in their place but I was very surprised by what I heard come out of her mouth.

"Oh yeah I see him buy panties here all the time, he is a down and out Sissy Man." She told them.

They all laughed and as they left they turned and waved good bye to me repeating over and over again how I was such a sissy.

It was now my turn at the cashier and I gave her a look and then spoke my mind.

"Why would you do something like that? Why would you basically turn on me and throw me under the bus like that?" I asked her.

"Oh don't worry about them, they are harmless, they are just busy bodies, you don't have to worry about them, I just gave them what they wanted to hear, I had no idea if you were wearing panties or not, but they weren't going to shut up until they got something to chew on and I just gave it to them." She said.

She took a breath and then continued.

"I think it is kind of hot that you are a sissy panty boy, I bet your cock gets hard pretty quickly when you have panties on all that silk and lace wrapping your cock up tight and snug."

"The people you have to worry about are other men who are not as secure in their own femininity as you are, you see they get scared by what you are doing, evidently they seem to think that someone will force them to do it as well, which you and I know is just ridiculous. They are the ones that get mean and not in that good way of holding you down or tying you up and spanking your sissy little ass. No they will hurt you physically."

"Now I kind of like you, and even a little more now that I know you are all female under your clothes and all, so if you ever need any help with anything including your shopping you just come and find me and I will give you a hand."

I looked back twice at her as I walked away from the register, she giggled at me the second time I looked and pointed at me though lower then my face, I looked down to see the bulge in my pants, I hadn't even noticed my cock getting hard, but it sure felt good against the material of the silky panty I had on today.

When I got into the car my wife noticed the bulge in my trousers as well and asked immediately about it.

I explained to her how embarrassed and humiliated I had felt by the two women who were making fun of me, but I felt just as embarrassed and humiliated when the cashier treated me like the sissy husband I am.

When I completed my story to her and looked up at her she had a big smile on her face.

"It's ok my dear that is exactly the way you are supposed to feel, it is that feeling right in between being made fun of and being controlled sexually by another that is the perfect place for a sissy panty boy. We want you to feel good and naughty but you should also have to pay for the privilege in a way that makes you inferior to the female species. "

I nodded understanding what she meant and actually agreeing with her on a deep level.

She continued.

"I am thinking I am going to take a larger role in your life my dear, I do hope you were not thinking of turning back now, the power of controlling you courses through my veins like a powerful drug."

I nodded now not understanding what she meant and actually fearing the consequences of what I began and thought to have been decided upon already.

My wife took up researching things on the Dominant Female role in relationships. She often informed me that she wanted to make sure she did everything right and didn't want to rush things more so then they needed to be for her own pleasure and amusement.

She came into the room and sat me down and said.

"I think we should have another conversation about your cross dressing."

"Yes my love" I responded.

"Up till now you have been very good, but I think for me to really get off we are going to have to add something to the little game we are playing with each other."

I wasn't really sure what she meant and gave her that look as if asking her to go on.

"She this is exactly what I was going to bring up, you are not openly insubordinate to me, but you do it in your own subtle way, a way that I can very easily see through but up till now really had no way to rectify the issue with you. But now I do."

"I want to bring corporal punishment into our game, this way if you do something that I feel is wrong I get to punish you in any way that I like, I mean we can establish a guideline of sorts but I promise to be fair about the punishments I hand out to you."

She told me.

There wasn't really much I could do about it I mean I had already given her the power she was just asking me for permission to use this new found idea of hers.

I smiled up at her.

"I think you are right my love, I think you should have a recourse with me if you feel I am being improper"

She smiled back.

"Good since you just gave me that look before I think we shall start with you over my knee for a good old fashion spanking."

She said.

She padded her knees which I had not noticed were already in position to receive me, as I slowly started to go over her knee she stopped me and informed me that I would go across her knees with only panties or naked never with pants. I undid my pants and exposed my bright pink silky hipsters, these exposed my soft cheeks which was what was coming next.

I felt her hand go across the panty material and then across my goose pimpled skin.

She hadn't told me how many times she was going to spank my ass, and it began with some much unexpected harsh swats to my ass cheeks. I hadn't remembered very well how much pain the human hand could inflict upon the soft part of your rear end but evidently it was quite a lot.

I had lost count at around twenty as she told me about how red my butt was now from her administrations, she also didn't fail to mention that her moistness level had increased and she was feeling very aroused in beating me in this fashion. In fact the only thing that was missing was a direct connection to the humiliation aspect of it.

Then the doorbell rang.

Without even a hesitation my wife spoke up.

"The door is open come on in"

My heart stopped, it was like everything became slow motion as I heard the click of the knob, watched it as it turned slowly, seeing the door move past its stationary position, the light burst into the room and was blinding and I couldn't make out who it was that was stepping into my home.

All I could think about was that I was across my wife's knees with my buttocks pink or more likely red from her spanking it while wearing a pair of pink hipsters.

I couldn't look but at the same time I was so compelled to see who was going to see me in this very awkward position.

As I strained to see the face, it looked familiar but I couldn't tell the tears had welled up as my wife continued beating my ass in a more ferocious manner.

"Oh my..."

That was what I heard as I saw our next door neighbor standing in our homes entrance.

This was followed by

"Well I never..."

"Do I truly see what I see?"

"Milady is that your husband across your knees and wearing a fine pair of pink panties on top of all that."

With my mind racing about how this all seemed and was in fact allowing the horse to leave the barn in a way since someone outside of our household and in our circle of friends now knew of my little fetish. What was worse was the fact that he didn't seem to be excusing himself and leaving.

"Oh dear look our lovely neighbor now knows of your little panty fetish." She laughed.

The tears continued to roll down my cheeks as my neighbor continued to come closer to me and my plight.

"Look how red you have made his ass cheeks." He told her.

"No look at how hard his cock is inside his panties, he likes to be embarrassed and I am sure your presence is exceeding levels of humiliation that he didn't even realize that he had within him."

She opened up her legs and revealed to my neighbor my hard cock.

"Isn't he pretty" she asked the neighbor.

"He most certainly is, would it be ok if I took a turn" asked me neighbor.

"Why that is a wonderful idea, go right ahead, let us see if you can make him cry" she giggled.

The neighbor's stroke was very different from my wife's stroke, and the smack of his hand against my panty covered ass cheek rang out through the house and made me yelp. The sheer force of his spanks began to move me back and forth my wife's lap, this in turn my cock on the silky soft material with just a little lace which was currently up against the underside of the head of my penis.

Over and over again his hand came down upon my ass, I was actually surprised how strong he was and my wife was getting even more excited as she exclaimed on how much redder he was able to make my cheeks. As he reached twenty of his own stroked I began to feel an equal level of arousal from the other side of where my body was being punished. My cock began to erupt through my panties and dripping on my wife's foot and high heel shoe.

"Well look at that"

My wife stopped the neighbor from continuing to spank me.

"You not only made him cry but your spanking also made him cum all over my shoe."

"Who would have thought that a spanking could make someone orgasm like that"

The neighbor thanked my wife for letting him a turn and hoped he could be involved in the future if she wished it.

I was sure that was not the last time we were going to see him.

She pushed me off her knee once the neighbor had left, I was on the ground my face inches from her shoe. She brought the shoe closer the tip just entering my mouth.

"Look what you have done, you have put your dirty cum on my shoe. You are going to lick it off my shoe right now."

My tongue slid up the shiny shoe tip capturing my cum that had dribbled from her foot on to her shoe.

"Look at you now, you won't be able to sit down for a while I'm afraid, but I am sure you enjoyed cumming without touching your pathetic little cock."

Her foot slid out of the shoe and I continued to lick up my stray cum that had fallen from the material of my panties and onto her lovely body.

When she was satisfied there was no more of my cum on her body or the floor, her legs opened revealing her flower to him, she was clean shaven and was obviously moist as it glistened on her inner lips. I did not have to be told and came to be between her legs and kissed her lips as if begging her permission to begin one of my favorite activities.

I knew her hands being on the back of my head were her indication for me to proceed.

I began with up licks until I felt her lips begin to part from the pressure of my tongue, as I continued to lick her clit my tongue would push into her and then would rise to her the button which brought her an amazing level of pleasure.

Taking her clit into my mouth and pulling at it with the suction of my mouth brought her up and aware in the way she was sitting. The pressure of her hands on the back of my head became even more persistent, and with the aid of my finger I was able to penetrate her and rub that spot in and up from her opening that could literally send a woman to a far off distant place if appropriately fondled.

I was able to do this to her today and was rewarded with a rare thing, that of the female ejaculation.

I had to admit I wasn't really ready for it when it first occurred, and then I thought that she had urinated on my face, but from her expression above me I knew in an instant that what had hit me in the face was not her piss at all.

Later that night I was rewarded and she rubbed lotion into my still very sore buttocks and even played with my cock until it got hard and allowed me to jerk myself off on her tits. Once I ejaculated though I once again had to lick it all off of her body. It was about then I noticed that she stopped calling me dear and referred to me solely as her sissy.

It continued like that for quite a while, she would often find small infractions that she would feel were worthy enough for her to beat me. I found the beatings quite intensive at first but I also found myself wanting her to spank me more and more, it felt so good to give myself over to her.

I was at this point in a bra and panties under my male clothes full time now, she liked that but she wanted me to do more.

She had shown me online some new herbal pills that she wanted me to try as they were designed to increase a woman's breast size. She thought it would be very good if I could fill out my small bra. We had sent away for them and began a regiment of following to the letter the instructions that were said to be guaranteed. After the third bottle of pills we saw no difference what so ever, she was heartbroken she so wanted me to have slightly larger breasts. The weird thing about it was that so did I, I wanted her to touch my bra and cup my young tender breasts like I was a new flowering young woman. The funny thing was that once I stopped taking these pills, my breasts became very tender, and then they became very soft and low and behold one morning I was putting my bra on before my shirt and I realized that my bra was filled with new breasts.

She played with them all day I liked it when she cupped them and fondled the nipples pinching them slightly, after a while they became very tender to the touch. Then she pinched them some more she thought it was exquisite that she had found a new way to torture me.

"I think it would be better if you being a little sissy and all especially now that your breasts are starting to grow, that you begin to where stockings full time as well. I know that you were not exactly interested in the stockings in the beginning and I didn't push the matter but moving forward I am going to want you to in ladies shoes and to facilitate that you will have to be used to wearing stockings."

Later that night I found myself with my legs in stockings and high in the air as my wife was assuming a position usually reserved for myself. She seemed very intrigued about being in that position. She had tied my hands to the back of the headboard and roughly pushed my bra up exposing my young breasts and she began sucking on my nipples. They were still sore from playtime earlier in the day but she didn't care too much and I felt her bite down on them and I would scream out. This of course was exactly what she wanted and would bite down even harder.

I hadn't noticed it at first but she was now gyrating on my crotch with her own. Well that is not exactly correct, she was pulling her hips back and then ramming them into my crotch, my balls which were held tightly to my body were getting rammed with her pelvis. It hurt and I would gasp out loud when she would ram her pelvis into me like she was penetrating me with my legs up in the air.

"How would you feel if I bought myself a strap on, you know one of those big fake cocks that are on the harness that a woman could wear if she wanted to see what it was like to have a much larger cock than her husband?"

"I am not sure I mean that how big of a cock are you going to get?" I asked her.

"That doesn't really matter, but if I did I would want to fuck you with it, you wouldn't have any problems with that would you?" She asked.

"No actually I think it might be kind of interesting, I always enjoyed when you would put your finger up my ass when you used to suck on my cock"

I smiled at her.

"Yay, about that, I don't think I am going to be sucking on your cock anymore, I think it is time you got over you're feeling about your own personal orgasm. "

"What do you mean" I asked her.

"It is not about you anymore sissy, I know you take care of all the laundry now and you do all the chores around the house and all, but I don't think that earns you the right to a blowjob or anything like that. Maybe we need to change your reward system, if you do really good I will fuck you gently with the strap on, and if you do badly I will fuck you harshly with the strap on."

It didn't seem like I was going to have an upside on this decision.

"Well then I will moan like the little slut that I am when you slide that strap on into my ass for the first time."

"There that's better I knew you would come around to my way of thinking."

The one thing she failed to mention was that she had already had gone to the store and picked up a strap on that she felt was appropriate, this I found out later when we were getting ready for bed.

With the stockings being a fairly new addition to my wardrobe, it was thought I should sleep in them as well since it would allow me time to become more accustomed to it was what she said, but in reality she had other ideas.

My eyes were brought specifically to her crotch, or I should say what was hanging from her crotch.

"What do you think sissy, are you ready to accept a new man in the house?"

I watched her wrap her hand around this thing, it extended in both directions from her closed hand, her hand would have engulfed the shaft of my cock.

"I don't know about that it is huge."

"It may be long but it is soft and I will lubricate your asshole so it slides right into you. I am going to so enjoy sliding it into you, you do realize that."

I knew full well I could picture her above me while doing it.

"Get those panties off, I want to take a look at your man pussy."

I pulled my knees up still not fully committed to the idea of her putting that eleven inches anywhere near my asshole. In a way pulling my panties down and removing them was buying me time to figure out a way out of this.

Unfortunately there really wasn't a way out of the predicament I found myself in and with panties being thrown on to the floor besides the bed she got on the bed and flopped her big rubber cock onto my crotch.

"Go ahead and touch it, it is very soft material and I think you will find it not so big that you cannot take it my little sissy."

I had to admit it didn't feel at all like what I thought it would feel, it felt very much like a real cock, well at least it felt like my own cock.

She took the tube of lube and squirted it out on her fingers, and they immediately disappeared from view and I felt them on the outside of my asshole and then one finger just pushed on into me. It surprised me at first, sure we had done that before I just didn't realize how eager she was to penetrate me to burst my anal cherry with her large strap on.

"Oh look at that two fingers in you now, I think once you are loose enough for three then I think you will be ready to take the man of the house, I think that is what we will call the strap on from now on. Whenever I want to fuck you in the ass I will tell you to go get the man of the house."

She laughed heartily on that, and I had to admit it was a good play on words, of course then I felt her third finger open me up a little more and now I knew the man of the house wouldn't be far behind, in fact he would be in my behind.

Once the third finger was in me she was in and out two or three times and then withdrew completely. What I felt next was the head of the man of the house. She was rubbing it up and down my well lubricated asshole.

"Look how your asshole puckers to receive the man of the house."

"I am going to fuck you until you cum like a young lady, you are going to have convince me of who you really are if you want to be able to sit down tomorrow from what I am going to give to you if you don't.

It was then that the head of her cock stopped moving and was directly at the opening of my asshole. Slowly I felt her push the head into me.

"Oh yay, there it is, my little sissy is getting his asshole opened today by a big cock, by the man of the house."

She did stop once the head had opened my anus to the maximum diameter of the girth of the strap on.

Her fingers now worked her way up my bare chest, she could feel my nipples through the material of the bra, and she smiled at me when she felt how hard they were.

"Oh look you like having you like having the man of the house in you don't you."

I couldn't help but nod my head, for the feeling was amazing.

She began to pinch my nipples harder twisting them to the right and the left.

Without warning without any sign from her she slid the man of the house into me fully in one push.

I felt like I jumped out of my body, before I could even get a chance to recover she withdrew the man of the house and once again had it slid back into me as she arched her hips to get the maximum force in my direction.

The sound that came out of my mouth as she repeatedly slid that large rubber cock into my asshole was unidentifiable; and it certainly wasn't a masculine sound that was for certain.

Her mouth was soon upon me I could feel the heat of her breath upon my face, her fingers still nimbly pinching and twisting my nipples.

All I could do was to receive her tongue as it probed into my own, she was penetrating me on a number of levels some I would not know of for a long time to come, but this date, this time would mark a place upon the time line of my transformation as the date that I took a full step into a world that was far from where I was.

She continued to penetrate me.

"Oh look how you like that big cock in your ass, look at you holding your legs up and see how pretty they look in the black stockings, the thigh highs are what you should wear all the time as it allows me access to your private parts without having to take them off. I like how they feel on my shoulders as I push the man of the house deeper inside of you."

I barely heard her; things began to spin in my brain, as I directed my thoughts to the feeling of a phallus inside of me filling me in a place I never really associated with pleasure upon my body. Being filled and hearing my wife talking dirty to me as she drove that cock into me was too much.

The warm wet feeling of my semi hard cock shooting a load of cum onto my bare belly, I heard her laughing as she withdrew the man of the house.

"Look at you, that is the second time you have had an orgasm without touching yourself, I guess I can lock it away and since you are dressing more and more like a girl I guess the only way you should be allowed to cum is by performing sexual acts that a girl would do."

I nodded my head as my cum began to fill my belly button.

The next day I woke up to find a butt plug on the night stand. I was familiar with the use of a butt plug and finding the lube still on the end table I used a little and worked the butt plug in until it was seated well inside of me, it was not the same feeling of being filled by the man of the house, but this toy kept my doorway from closing completely which turns out is something that allows her to enter you anytime she feels like it without much foreplay.

I fitted a new pair of panties; these were clingy boy shorts, a pinkish purple color, they had a matching bra, and of course the new thigh highs were so much fun to put on. I had been shaving my legs well pretty much my whole body for quite a while now so the feeling of putting on stockings always made me feel special and pretty.

"Let me check to make sure you have it in all the way."

I unceremoniously bent over so she could pull my panties down and the jolts that went through my body were very measurable in my opinion. When she turned the plug a full three hundred and sixty degrees while inside of me, and then gave it a good push, and up came the panties and then a swat on my butt told me I was ready for the day.

Turning back around I was ready to make my way to the kitchen so I could begin my daily chores, what I saw was a pair of four inch heels black patent leather, with an ankle strap. I stepped into them and was in like a different world all together, I was four inches higher, yes, but I was afraid to take a step as I figured I would break my ankle within the first half an hour.

What I didn't realize is that when I stepped into them and she fixed the ankle strap I heard a click and when her hands moved I realized I was just pad locked into the first shoe, it took a moment to register but when it did the second click let me know that I was one step too late to do anything about it.

"Good, I have wanted to put you in heels for so long had to get past the stockings step."

"Aren't you glad that I changed my mind and decided to be involved in the complete feminization of you, I want you to feel just how fun and exciting it is to be a woman, well not really, but I get to enjoy watching you suffer."

I once again went about my way to start my chores, and I was truly amazed at the difference four inches changes everything you do. I had to slow down so much so that I wouldn't hurt myself, I didn't want to have too much over confidence and fall on my ass.

The chores in the kitchen seemed like they took forever, she was getting kind of upset with me for taking so long but I just couldn't seem to get the hang of the heels and the one time I tried to pick up the pace I found myself on my backside not realizing exactly how I got there, she thought that was hilarious. I however found it very painful as the impact drove the butt plug deeper into my asshole. Once I was able to actually get on my feet I had to do a reach around just to make sure the plug hadn't gone all the way into me. I was relieved to feel the plug was still where it should be. Once the kitchen was done it was off to be on my hands and knees as I cleaned the bathrooms, she liked watching me on my hands and knees often times telling me to stick my butt higher in the air. It was during those times that I would feel the sting of her belt across my backside. She loved the way I would jump when the belt made contact. This simple reaction would get her so excited she would often stop my chores just so I could lick her pussy. "Come over now my little sissy bitch time for you to make me cum." She would grin at me.

There I would be still on my hands and knees as she would lift her skirt and press my face into her wet pussy, with my hands still in the cleaning gloves from the seventies, she would guide my head with one hand and expose her clitoris so I would be able to find it quite easily and bring her to orgasm quickly. It would not take long and soon I would feel her shake and then she would start to moan and I knew she was quietly singing out to a higher power.

"You are so good with your tongue, much better with your tongue then your sissy dick"

The slap that came next across my face caught me off guard because of the surprise of it but also because of the force behind it.

"Now get back to work you little sissy, your chores are taking too long and you are going to have to be punished because of this." She said as she walked away.

I finished up the bathrooms quickly since I didn't have to stand in those heels to do it; I guess being down on my hands and knees actually did have an advantage after all. I gave a wry smile once that thought slowly drifted from my mind.

The laundry was next and having to bend down to get the laundry from the dryer was excruciating on my toes which felt like they had been tied tightly together with ropes as they were continuously forced into an ever decreasing space within these shoes.

Luckily there was only one load in the dryer and I was able to make quick work of the folding and the hanging up of the necessary items. I gave a slight smile to myself as I hung the last blouse up in the closet as I realized that though it was my wife's blouse I had been the one to wear it last.

The smile slipped away as I turned to see her standing there in the doorway of the closet holding the thick leather paddle which had the word bitch embossed into the outer layer. It never left the word on my backside but she always tried to leave it there when she had the opportunity.

"Since you took so long in getting your chores done today you will not be given the opportunity to have an orgasm, maybe next time you will work harder for something that you want. "

She stepped to the side allowing me to walk slowly out of the closet, what I was presented with in our bedroom was some ropes tied to each corner of the bed. Standing before the bed I was told to lay down keeping my feet on the ground. She quickly tied my hands to the corners at the headboard making sure to pull my arms tight. Next she kicked my legs apart further and further which was very difficult in the heels I was in.

"I don't know how far I can do that in these shoes" I told her. She didn't appreciate my input and I found my ankles at a very awkward and uncomfortable angle as she tied them tightly to the headboard.

My panties were simply cut off of my body, which actually made me sad as I really liked those panties, when I told her that she simply rolled them into a ball and stuffed them into my mouth.

My balls now hung freely and I became very frightened when I felt the leather paddle tapping them gently, I knew I was not ready for anything severe to happen to my balls, I had seen videos and they intrigued me but we had never really played with that yet so I was quickly becoming scared as the gentle tapping became a little more and then a little more still. Each time the paddle connected with my balls it would make me jump and she would laugh.

"Are you afraid I am going to ruin your balls, I could you know, if I were to damage your balls you wouldn't really be anything of a man after that, would you?" she asked.

Obviously I couldn't respond with the panties in my mouth so she simply just kept playing with them, when she had enough fun with the balls I felt her slip a rope around them and she snugged my balls downward and evidently tied that to the bed as well.

"Now I am going to beat you until I feel satisfied, I wouldn't jump to much since your balls are tied off and you don't want to rip them from your body." She laughed.

That first slap on my right cheek was fast and firm and I did jump and realized just how little room I had for movement which meant that I was going to have to take this beating full on without any way of absorbing the blows other than full force.

I quickly lost count and was sure my ass cheeks were blood red and in fact when the beating stopped and she came around to where I could see her she showed me the paddle and how there was blood on it where it had broken the skin.

"Well look at those tears, are you crying from a little paddling?" She asked

I nodded my head and knew that the tears were flowing quite steadily down my face.

Well now that you have paid the price for taking so long to do your chores, I have a little treat for you tonight.

She released the rope that held my balls which allowed me a little more movement, next I felt a plug being put back inside of me which was out of the norm she usually would get the Man of the House and do me good up the ass.

When I felt the plug begin to vibrate at a very high speed I felt my cock begin to grow, and then I felt her putting a condom on my cock. I knew something was very different at that, and then I felt her put a rubber band around the base of the condom.

She was looking at me again.

"I want you to know what is going on right now. That plug will continue to vibrate making your cock get hard and then it will get soft and then it will get hard again, you won't be able to concentrate on anything else but the fact that your butt is vibrating. Each time your cock gets hard it will slowly dribble out some of that large amount of cum that is just sitting in your big blue balls. I was invited out for a drink this evening; evidently our neighbor thinks I am quite the woman to put you in your place and would like to show his appreciation for me with drinks and some good conversation. I know you are thinking about it and I am going to tell him how you are tied up I know this will humiliate you even further. By the time I get home I am sure the condom will have an ample supply of your cum that you will get a good mouthful of it before I untie you and go to bed."

I looked at her and another tear rolled down my cheek.

"Oh don't worry silly I still love you and I always will love you, you have opened up a new world for me and I am going to truly enjoy every single bit of it, I doubt the neighbor is going to be even worth my time, but I figured it would be worth the date with him just to see your face knowing that our neighbor knows just what kind of a man you really are."

Well I have to do go get ready for my date, those batteries are brand new so you will have a few hours of the strong vibrations until they wear down a little bit, oh and I almost forgot the egg is going to probably get hot running continuously like that so don't worry it won't damage your asshole but I am sure you are going to think it is.

I heard the door to the room close and then open again as the lights in the room were turned out and then the door closed again and all was silent. Well silent except for the fact that my asshole was vibrating franticly as my cock became hard and I felt a little cum ooze out of the head of my cock and into the reservoir tip of the condom.

My mind began to race, it was one of the most amazing moments I had ever experienced up to that point in my life.

She was right after all my mind immediately focused on the vibrations in my asshole, I couldn't focus on anything for very long at all, every time I thought about my wife being out with another man my mind would jump back to the fact that she had plugged my asshole and then I felt my cock growing hard. I tried not to think of this man touching my wife, but I knew she was looking forward to having him do just that. They probably held hands as they walked to some dark club or something like that. He was probably dancing with her and touching her breasts through her clothing. She was probably rubbing up on him.

I couldn't tell if my cock was leaking cum into the condom or not but my cock began to get soft again, as I felt feelings of humiliation as I was tied to the bed with a plug up my ass while my wife was out enjoying her evening with another man. Again my mind raced to the vibrations in my asshole, she was right it felt like the plug was getting warm from the little motor of the vibrator going for so long a time.

What if they were sitting in a booth talking and listening to the music, we would always enjoy talking to each other when we were out, could she be enjoying the conversation of this other man more than me. He could be sitting so close next to her probably with his hand upon her leg, slowly working his hand up her inner thigh, and she would be letting him, probably smiling at him as his fingers came closer and closer to her prize.

My cock started getting rock hard again thinking about his fingers so close to her pussy, the way she was talking when she left she would probably open her legs and pull her panties to the side and let him finger her right there in the club under the table. She was probably rubbing his hard cock through his pants as well just to see how large it was.

Got the vibrator was driving me nuts, it was getting into my mind and I couldn't think of anything but the endless sexual possibilities of what could be happening this evening.

What if the conversation was about me, what if she was telling him how she had left me and what she had been doing to me, or even worse what she wants to do to me down the road, she seemed liked she really enjoyed me being feminized that she liked seeing me in panties and stockings full time, even the bra was her idea after all. My cock was getting hard again. She was probably setting the hook right then and there telling him how she needed a real man to fuck her now since I was going to be her sissy husband after all that she was going to need a real cock, since she wasn't going to be fucked by some sissy. Sissies after all were just that, more a girlfriend who needed to be controlled and punished then a man who deserved to fuck you.

Oh my god I thought to myself, this was her way of milking me so I would get no pleasure from an orgasm and would relieve myself of the cum that was building up in my balls. I realized my cock was hard once again.

This went on for quite some time between thinking about what crazy and sexual thing she was doing with a stranger to what she was planning on doing with me was driving me crazy, and each time I let my mind run off in some deranged direction my cock would get hard.

By the time the batteries finally started to die, I couldn't count the amount of times my cock became hard, but it seemed like it happened a hundred or so times.

Later that night when I heard her open the bedroom door she didn't say a word but pulled the plug out of my numb ass from all the vibrating and started to laugh.

"I guess you should know that I didn't go out I was in the other room watching television, but I wanted to plant that seed in your head, because it could very well happen. I truly feel like I am free to do whatever I want to do and the fact that you are not the man of the house any more by any means if I want to have sex with other men since you obviously are not up to the challenge as a man then I will do just that. Do you understand me?"

"Yes ma'am I realize that you are in charge and will do whatever it is you seem fit, I am your little sissy and will abide by whatever it is you want me to do."

"Good you can't understand how happy I am to hear you say that sweetheart"

She began to work the condom off of my now soft cock, I felt her pull it free and she brought it around in front of me so I could see.

"Look at how much I got out of your balls from just the thought of me having sex with another man"

I couldn't believe it the reservoir tip was over flowing there must have been what amounted to three or four full loads of cum in the condom.

"Since you obviously like the idea of me fucking other men and since you are worthless sissy it is time for you open up and drink you cum down."

I couldn't believe what she wanted me to do but I watched as she brought the condom up to my mouth, I could smell the cum it smelled like sex. I knew I didn't have much of a choice but I couldn't believe I was going to drink that much cum.

"You need to learn to love it, sweetheart, after all if I start fucking other men you can bet I am going to be bringing home my pussy with all there cum inside for you to lick out of me."

I started to protest that idea but she was too quick and upturned the condom and my mouth filled with my salty sticky cum.

When she bent down to kiss me and I felt her tongue enter my mouth swirling with cum I could feel my cock getting hard again.

She had decided that some regular routines would be good for me, so on the week nights I was always in stockings, panties and a bra, and she would pick out some dress or outfit she would want me when I got home from work. Sometimes it was a simple dress or maybe a skirt and a blouse, she had dressed me up in capris with sensible shoes so I could do the house work one night, other times it was a French maid outfit, that was when I knew she would be getting the "Man of the house" out and I would be bent over something while she enjoyed herself.

Now on the weekends that were a totally different thing, on the weekends I would be expected to do my hair or don my wig and apply full make up, she would help me but eventually I was going to have to be able to do it myself. If she felt like it we would go out to dinner or something very public.

Of course I never had any say in the matter what so ever.

One weekend we decided to go to dinner and a movie, she had me dressed very provocatively and we were attracting the eyes of a number of young hunks in the restaurant and even in line for the movie tickets. She had begun flirting with this one guy who was with his friends, he was big and tall and very muscular, I was playing the shy one because I was still very nervous about being out in public. Of course she mentioned some rather nasty things about me to this big hunky guy. In the theatre the group of young men was sitting in a totally different row from us and I had thought that was that.

The movie hadn't started yet and we were simply waiting.

"Hey I am going to go and get us a snack."

I didn't think much about it, and she was gone for a little while the lights had gone down and the previews were on the screen when she came back. She hadn't brought anything from the concession stand but she did have the young hunk in tow with her and she sat him right down between us.

I looked at her like asking what she was doing.

She smiled at me.

"I thought you might like a little cock with your movie"

She undid his zipper and reached over and put my hand on his cock which was extremely large.

"Come on get down on your knees and if you suck well enough you will get a surprise"

I couldn't say no to her it was against the rules, all I could do was look at her in total humiliation as I slowly with my hand on this guy's hard cock get between his knees and as the movie started so did I taking the head of his cock in my mouth.

I missed the first fifteen minutes of the movie but I did get my surprise eventually as I felt his hands on the back of my head holding my head on his cock as he pumped his load into my mouth and down my throat.

He didn't hang out after that but went back to his friends.

She laughed and giggled as I had nothing to drink to get the taste of his cum out of my mouth.

"That popped into my mind I was so sure you would put up a fight but I guess you really are just a little sissy submissive bitch. I am going to have so much more fun knowing I can make you do just about anything"

I had already missed a good portion of the movie and didn't really know what was going on when she then instructed me to get down between her legs and lick her until she came.

I hadn't realized how sticky the floor was the first time being so caught up in the moment this time however I noticed everything.

She picked up her legs and separated them wide for me putting her heels on the seats in front of her. If anybody looked over this way they would have realized right away what was going on, she certainly wasn't trying to be inconspicuous about it.

I began to lick her, and she sat back and enjoyed the rest of the movie laughing and pushing my head into her pussy I must have made her cum three times but she would not let me out from between her legs until the movie credits were rolling up the screen.

I quickly got back into my seat with my face looking like a glazed donut as the lights came up.

I had really wanted to see the movie and was somewhat disappointed in not getting the chance to watch it, but who was I to say anything after all this was what I had wanted my whole life, was to be nothing more than a little sissy slut.

When she saw my cock rock hard after the experience which was very awkward with the dress I was in at the time she realized that this was going to present a problem.

"We are going to need to find a way to ensure that your cock doesn't get hard while you are dressed like a woman"

We had to wait a few moments after everyone filed out of the theatre before we could safely leave without me standing out, literally.

The night the neighbor came over for dinner I was totally caught off guard as I was never told so when I answered the door in the French maid outfit I was taken aback seeing him standing at the door with flowers in his hand. He simply swept past me giving me a good look over.

"My you do look like the pretty sissy slut don't you?"

I simply nodded

"I really like what you have done with your body, I am going to ask the Misses if you can come over and clean my home for me and do my household chores"

My wife soon arrived and greeted him accepting his flowers and taking him by the hand and bringing him to the couch.

"Go get us some drinks" she told me.

I was not allowed to sit and they spoke about me as if I was not there.

"So how is it coming along with your little sissy?"

"Oh she is doing well, the other day I had him sucking cock at the movie theatre"

The both laughed out loud at that

"Get out of here in public"

"Yup then I made him go down on me as well, he never even saw the movie. Oh and get this his cock was rock hard by when he was done we had to wait for his pitiful cock to get soft before we could leave."

Another big laugh by both of them.

"So what is next for him?" he asked.

"I was thinking it was time to have him watch me get fucked by a real man"

"Oh are you going to cuckold him as well as make him a sissy?"

"He needs to know his new place in the batting line up"

"Did you have anybody in mind for that one" He asked her.

"Well why do you think you are here"

The conversation ended right there and they began to kiss, not pecking at each other but warm wet luscious kisses tongues probing and searching, right there in front of me as I stood there in my fishnet stockings and my poufy French maid skirt.

It didn't take very long before his hands were on her tits and hers were in his crotch. He pushed her down on the couch and ripped her blouse open revealing my wife's ample bosom. He began to suck on her nipples licking them and nibbling on them. He was being very rough with her and she liked it. Her hands were still working the outside of his pants making his cock full and hard. She had the belt undone and the buttons as well as they slid down his legs. I had a great view of his ass as he scooted up and shoved his large cock into my wife's mouth. His knees were up to her armpits as the back of her head was in the corner of our couch as she tried to take his massive manhood deeper into her mouth. I couldn't believe that I was simply standing there watching this but I knew if was to interfere I would be severely beaten for my transaction.

With his cock already rock hard the blowjob attempt was merely for lubricating his hard shaft with her saliva and he withdrew from her mouth and raised her legs without ado he lined his ten inch cock up with her opening and slid it all the way into her. She screamed for being stretched so rapidly but he didn't care he liked to hear her scream and withdrew and did it again.

It didn't take long for her to accept his shaft as her own lubrication was kicking in full gear as I watched the stain on the corner of the couch grow from her wetness. He fucked her good ramming his cock into her.

"Do you see this" I heard her scream

"Are you watching your wife get fucked by a real man"

"With a real cock"

This was all about her though and she quickly gave up on trying to humiliate me further then I already was and went back to enjoying the attention the very large cock was giving to her.

My own cock was rock hard pushing on my panties, I wanted to reach down and stroke it while he fucked her but I dare not.

I scooted to the side a little bit so I could see her face and what I saw was something my cock never had done before to her, she arched her head back and rolled her eyes in the back of the head and the neighbor pounded her pussy with his large cock. I knew she was going to be sore for a few days after this fucking.

He continued consistently for about a half an hour of just pounding away at her, I lost count of the amount of times that she said something degrading about me and my performance as a man and what a pitiful piece of shit cock I had and then she would cum again and forget all about me.

When he finally did cum, he pulled his cock out and sprayed his cum all over her wet and soaked crotch, it was like she stuck her pussy into a birthday cake it was so covered with his cream.

He sat back next to her and I offered him his drink which he raised his glass to me and drank from deeply.

I turned to her and she was slowly coming back to reality and looked at the cum all over her pussy and simply pointed at it and told me to clean it up.

I was down on my knees and began to lick her pussy swallowing the neighbors cum in the process.

"Is it ok if I use my belt on him while he is doing that" he asked her.

"Oh yes that would be lovely nothing like a little pain with his humiliation"

With my ass in the air and my face busy licking up another man's cum from my wife's pussy I felt my panties pulled down exposing my ass in my French maid outfit. The first stroke of his belt across my ass stung and made me jump by she took hold of my head and held it right where she wanted to as he strapped my ass over and over again until I began to scream into her pussy and the tears began to roll down my face. He was brutal I had thought I was going to like him but now I was kind of scared of him. I didn't know how many times he whipped me with his big leather belt but I knew I wouldn't be sitting the rest of the night that was for sure.

When he was done she told me to turn around and to thank him.

I could barely see him from the tears but when I turned around what was in my face was his cock and I got the impression he would rather not hear me say thank you. I took his soft cock in my mouth even soft it was huge and tasted of her pussy. He was not very gentle about it and he tried to push his cock deep down my throat which almost caused me to gag. I was still crying and I think he liked the idea of a crying beaten sissy husband sucking his cock because it go hard real fast.

He removed his cock from my mouth and pushed me back around to face her, she was smiling from what I could see from watery eyes and she took my hands and pulled me up close to her bosom. I thought she was going to comfort me as I felt her arms hug me tightly. The next thing I felt was the neighbors cock pushing against my asshole, and like before he didn't go gently but shoved it into me and I screamed as the pain shot through my body but she held me tightly as he began to pound my asshole just like he did her pussy.

I heard her whisper into my ear as he drove his ten inch cock up and into my ass all the way.

"Seems like there is a new man of the house."

A Note From the Author

Well here it is the end of another project, I get mixed feelings when I come to the end of a project, I enjoy writing so much that I am sad to be at the end but at the same time I know that now others will get a chance to experience my wonderful lustful and sometimes sadistic thoughts via the story or the assignment. I just have so much fun writing about the experiences I have with my own submissive play things, they are such good little boi's all dressed so pretty and they do whatever I ask of them, well they know they will be punished if they don't.

So now it is your turn to once again do what I ask of you.

I would like to hear from you, I am going to give you my personal email address so you can contact me so that I can get your feedback on the stories and the assignments and anything else you would like to tell me about. I would love to hear about your own stories and experiences, I just love it when I get email from the people who read my work, so don't hesitate to contact me, who knows maybe I will give you a special assignment just for you.

Write to me soon…….

Love

Mistress Jessica

Mistressjessica01@gmail.com

www.ingramcontent.com/pod-product-compliance
Lightning Source LLC
Chambersburg PA
CBHW070812290526
45795CB00002B/699